PORTSMOUTH AIRPORT

Anthony Triggs

HALSGROVE

First published in Great Britain in 2002

British Library Cataloguing in Publication Data

A CIP record for this book is available from the British Library

ISBN 1 84114 153 4

HALSGROVE
Halsgrove House
Lower Moor Way
Tiverton Devon EX16 6SS
T: 01884 243242
F: 01884 243325
www.halsgrove.com

Printed in Great Britain by Bookcraft Ltd, Midsomer Norton.

ACKNOWLEDGEMENTS

As always so many of my friends and colleagues have come forward with help.
I must thank my publisher Steven Pugsley, Peter Rogers, Sarah Quail, Tom Dethridge,
Ted Saunders, David Garvey, Ron Brown, Douglas White, Alf Harris, Roy Adams,
Don Upward of the Southampton Hall of Aviation, Paul Gladman of the Flight Collection,
and Bob Irwin of JA Hewes photographers for his darkroom expertise.
Lastly my wife Sue provides help and encouragement that far exceeds the few words
of thanks I can write here. Most of the pictures used are from my own collection
or from those of the people mentioned above, and while every effort has been made
to trace the source of a few others I must apologise in advance for any inadvertent omissions.

INTRODUCTION

'S'eventy years ago Portsmouth entered the air age, when in 1932, the city's municipal airport was opened – only the eighth of its kind in the country. Just four years earlier, in 1928, the Air Ministry had written to all towns and cities with a population of 20,000 or more, pointing out the advantages of having airport facilities, and the city fathers, to their credit, responded positively.

'Portsmouth must be the vanguard,' said one councillor at a meeting called to consider the feasibility of such a scheme, which immediately won approval. Already Blackpool, Hull, Norwich, Liverpool, Nottingham, Manchester and Bristol had applied for airport licences, and Portsmouth certainly was not going to be left straggling.

The seventy-six acre Highgrove Farm, in the north-eastern corner of Portsea Island was purchased for £37,000, but this area was not enough and negotiations were entered into to buy neighbouring government land, which included part of the old Napoleonic fortifications. Altogether the land purchase came to £77,000 for a total area of 276 acres.

The work, which was to cost the city a further £52,000 was put out to tender, and by 1931 things were really on the move. The ground, most of which was in a poor state, had to be drained, cleared and levelled. Much of the land was copse and many trees and hedges were cleared and ditches filled. More than 105,000 cubic yards of the old fortifications and thousands of tons of concrete were blown up before the land could be consolidated by heavy tractors, flattened and then seeded. The ultimate test stipulated that a car be driven over the ground with no signs of jolting.

The airport boasted a total area of 204 acres and had grass landing strips of 4500 ft and 2500 ft. Two hangars, a refreshment chalet, customs office and control tower were built, while the old farmhouse was cleverly converted into flying club premises. There was even provision for a tea lawn in the orchard.

In June 1931 before the aerodrome was complete, veteran flyer Charles W Scott flew in with newspaper columnist Hannen Swaffer. The pair were touring the country in Scott's Moth aircraft in which he made the record-breaking flight to Australia, and Swaffer was describing the tour to the avid readers of the *Daily Herald*.

One of the hangars was soon occupied. Portsmouth, Southsea and Isle of Wight Aviation had secured the rights for passenger services to the island and for joyrides, and by the end of June 1932 had already taken more than 1000 people into the air.

The Southsea department store of Handleys – now Debenhams – placed an advertisement in the *Evening News* announcing: 'We now sell aircraft.' The plane was a Redwing biplane costing £650. 'It is immensely strong and can land and take off in quite a small field,' the advertisement read.

The official airport opening was planned for 2 July 1932, and a great air pageant was planned, with aviation expert Captain Reginald Stocken as pageant master. He was full of praise for the new airport, saying: 'I consider the Portsmouth Aerodrome the best in the country, if not one of the best civil aerodromes in Europe.'

Despite the early light rain, on the day more than 50,000 excited spectators made their way across country to the airport for the afternoon's opening ceremony and air display. The official opening was originally expected to have been performed by the Minister for Air, the Marquis of Londonderry, but at the last minute he was forced to travel to Geneva for a conference, so in his absence the task was undertaken by the Under-secretary for Air, Sir Philip Sassoon.

In his address he said: 'By your courage you have set other towns and cities an excellent example, and in time those without aerodromes will realise their mistake.'

The crowd was then entertained by the air pageant in which more than 100 aircraft took part in the games and displays. Finally one of the highlights of the day took place. Special arrangements had been made for a visit by the giant German airship, the Graf Zeppelin. She flew in from Hanworth and arrived at Portsmouth by the evening, descending so low that members of the crew could be seen waving from the windows of the gondolas.

Two days later the airship's visit was the subject of a question in the Commons by Portsmouth North MP, Sir Bertram Falle. He was assured that the Zeppelin had not flown over any prohibited areas of Portsmouth, such as the dockyard. This did not convince many Portmuthians, who expressed even more doubts during the dark days of the Blitz.

One small but interesting feature of the opening day was two of the first freight deliveries. Firstly Fry's chocolate had obtained the contract for the sale of confectionery, and disdaining on such an occasion anything so mundane as delivery by road or rail, arranged for stocks to be flown to Portsmouth in a gaily-painted aircraft. Soon after, a parcel of Parker Duofold pens was delivered by the company's aircraft piloted by a Captain Preston, who brought the pens by air to meet the urgent request of the Southern Stationery Depot in Elm Grove, Southsea.

The *Evening News* with commendable foresight posed the question: 'Is this the beginning of commercial delivery services in this country?'

The great day was rounded off with a grand event at the Guildhall, where in the ballroom was hung a huge set-piece depicting an illuminated plane flying gracefully through the sun's rays.

A week later, on 8 July, the airport was firmly at the leading edge of the news again when it was chosen as the turning point for the King's Cup air race. The event consisted of two legs – the first of 738 miles and the second of 495 miles, and Portsmouth was the finishing point for each section.

It was declared that 10 August 1932 would be National Aviation Day. Another huge pageant was staged at the airport and air ace Sir Alan Cobham arrived with his flying circus. Sir Alan was impressed with Portsmouth and declared with great enthusiasm and doubtful grammar: 'It is about the best aerodrome I have landed in.'

At the same time a woman was providing the airport with its first large-scale record-breaking attempt and the worldwide publicity that went with it. The Hon Mrs Virginia Bruce already held the 24-hour speedboat record and the 24-hour British car record, and now was setting out to take the air endurance title as well. The record had already been set at 50hours 38minutes, and Mrs Bruce was aiming to beat this time.

She set out to do this in an Isle-of-Wight-built Saro Windhover seaplane – City of Portsmouth – but her support aircraft – a Bristol fighter and a Gipsy Moth – were to be flown from Portsmouth Aerodrome. After a false start when the aircraft's generator failed after 16 hours, she took off again from Cowes on 6 August and was eventually forced to make a crash landing at sea near Felixstowe after 54hours 13minutes – easily beating the record. The aircraft was subsequently sold to Jersey Airways and flew until 1938.

A year later Portsmouth entered the aviation history books when a company that was to have a great impact on both the city and the aircraft industry as a whole, moved to the airport. The Airspeed aircraft company had been formed in York in 1931 and was the brainchild of four men – Lord Grimthorpe, Alfred Hessell Tiltman, Sir Alan Cobham, and Nevil Shute Norway, later to become famous as the novelist Nevil Shute.

Portsmouth Airport was a very suitable location, being near Langstone Harbour, which had been designated a major terminal for flying boat services throughout the Commonwealth as soon as the new Short Empire craft were in service, a dream that never materialised. However Airspeed produced some of the finest aircraft of the time – the Envoy, Courier, Ferry, and the mainstay of the RAF, the Oxford. The company was taken over by de Havilland after the war, which in turn became part of the Hawker Siddeley empire.

In August 1933 International Airlines started a new service from Croydon to Portsmouth, Southampton and Plymouth but had discontinued the service in less than three weeks, however by December another company, Jersey Airways, commenced scheduled flights to Jersey, landing on the beach on the Channel island.

Portsmouth, Southsea and Isle of Wight Aviation had helped form the Portsmouth Aero Club, which on 6 September organised an Isle of Wight handicap race which was won by Sir Charles Rose flying a de Havilland Moth 60G. The following year the club's horizons expanded and two 'Round the Island' races were organised. The first was twice around the island, and the second a single circuit.

SIR ALAN COBHAM'S GREAT AIR DISPLAY

CITY AIRPORT PORTSMOUTH

TO-MORROW SATURDAY, 19th AUGUST

THE MOST THRILLING FLYING DISPLAY YET SEEN IN THIS COUNTRY

20 VARIED TYPES OF MODERN AIRCRAFT,
HIGH-SPEED AEROBATICS &
INVERTED FLYING IN FORMATION,
FAST FIGHTING MACHINES,
DUAL DELAYED-DROP PARACHUTE DESCENTS,
AUTOGIROS,   SENSATIONAL CRAZY FLYING,
3-ENGINED AIRLINERS,   DARING WING-WALKING.

TWO COMPLETE DISPLAYS AT 2.15 p.m. & 7 p.m.

Admission: **1/3;** Children **6d.;** Cars **1/-**

During 1933 Portsmouth led the world and installed simple passenger boarding gates, which were believed to be the first in the country – one for Shanklin passengers, one for those travelling to Ryde, and another for Shoreham. The last one was for pleasure flight passengers.

September 1934 saw Sir Alan Cobham's attempt to fly non-stop to Karachi, utilising his pioneering in-flight refuelling system which had been perfected in the skies above Portsmouth and the Solent. He flew in an Airspeed Courier – G-ABXN – and was aiming to refuel over Malta and Alexandria. A broken throttle linkage caused him to abandon the attempt at Malta but the attempt still paved the way towards the air-to-air refuelling techniques utilised today.

In August 1935 more than 10,000 people flocked to the airport to see that small is beautiful when French aviator Henri Mignet demonstrated his little *Pou du Ciel* – Flying Flea – aircraft, and in May of 1936 the daring birdman Clem Sohn displayed his sky-diving skills to a huge crowd. Both men were forced to take to their heels to avoid hordes of autograph hunters! Sohn sadly lost his life during a display at Vincennes, France, in 1937, aged just 26 years.

Portsmouth residents who were out of their beds early on 23 August 1936, were surprised to see a huge number of aircraft flying over the city. The Portsmouth Aero Club had staged a mock attack on the city where five club planes were taken up to defend against 32 raiders in a dawn patrol. Twelve planes got through the defences without having their registration numbers recorded! Afterwards pilots and passengers were entertained to breakfast in the chalet before they left for home.

In 1936 the airport hosted another long-distance air bid. In September the Portsmouth to Johannesburg air race was staged. The South African millionaire Isaac Schlesinger put up a total of £10,000 prize money, but the race was not a happy one. Out of the original 14 entries only nine faced the starting gun at Portsmouth, and only one finished the course. The great hope for Portsmouth was the first one away, Airspeed Envoy Gabrielle – number 13 in the race – which crashed in South Africa killing two of the four crew. Hundreds of people got up early and claimed vantage points at the airport to see the aircraft set off, starting at 6.30am.

With the outbreak of war Airspeed continued with the production of the Oxford, and built many of the Horsa gliders, so important during the D-Day invasion. With peace the airport resumed its normal operations, after the government lifted the restrictions for civilian flying. However in 1947 – with a large helping of *déjà vu* – an Avro Anson overshot the runway and ended up on the main Portsmouth to London railway line, shorting out the current. The occupants managed to get to safety before the plane caught fire.

As a celebration for the lifting of wartime restrictions Portsmouth Aero Club arranged an air display in May 1947 where many hundreds of people – most of whom had possibly seen too much of aircraft during the war – flocked to the airport. More than 200 aircraft arrived – many of them brand new. It was said that it was easier to acquire a new aircraft than it was to obtain a new car!

Soon Channel Airways had moved in and begun services to the Channel Island, at first using Dakotas, and then moving up to the turboprop Hawker Siddeley 748s. By the mid sixties the airport was handling more than 60,000 passengers a year and was designated a regional airport. On the strength of this a new terminal was built near the Eastern Road, with full customs facilities. However, in August 1967 all this was to change when a double disaster occurred. A golden-coloured 748 overran the field and aquaplaned into the bank on the north side of the airport. Less than ninety minutes later a second 748 suffered a similar lack of traction and ended up with its nose across the Eastern

Road. Permission to operate this type of aircraft was withdrawn, but for a few restrictive conditions, and basically the airport ceased to be a viable concern. Channel Airways flew on for a while using Herons and Doves, but eventually pulled out altogether.

The 'yo-yo' airport, as it was dubbed, remained devoid of commercial services until early in 1971, when a new company was formed to run the Channel Island routes again. JF Airlines was the brainchild of city councillor John Fisher, who had tried unsuccessfully to interest the council in a municipally-backed airline. He courageously resigned and started his own airline. In the March the company received permission from the Air Transport Licensing Board to operate eight daily flights to the Channel Islands.

A jubilant Mr Fisher said: 'This is the culmination of two years of hard campaigning for the airline, and it is going to put Portsmouth back on the aviation map.'

The company took delivery of its first aircraft – an 18-seat twin-engine Pioneer – which was described as 'the safest of planes with a safe reputation'. But by June 1972 John Fisher had stepped down as managing director, and the company had changed its name to Jersey Ferry Airlines, and the new owners planned to exchange the Pioneers with Herons. The first one – Spirit of Enterprise – was christened by actress Barbara Murray, who was at that time starring in the television series *The Planemakers*.

However, in the financial year ending March 1972 the airport suffered a loss of more than £9000, and the lights were beginning to dim on its financial future. It closed completely on 31 December 1973, leaving with it an historic legacy.

The site of Portsmouth Airport is now hidden by the homes of the Anchorage Park housing development, but a few names remain to remind us. A handful of businesses keep aeronautics alive, and a number of roads – Nevil Shute Road, Dundas Lane, Norway Road – serve to remind us of a great enterprise.

This short flight down memory lane is not intended to be a definitive history of the airport – I leave that to more able pens than mine – but provides an affectionate pictorial look at one of Portsmouth's greatest enterprises, which was also one of its biggest failures.

Anthony Triggs
Portchester, 2002

This rustic view of Highgrove Farm in the north-eastern corner of Portsea Island was soon to be a thing of the past in the name of progress after the city council purchased 300 acres of land, including the 76-acre farm and allotments, to provide for what was then called the municipal aerodrome.

Left: Highgrove farmhouse, also seen in the previous picture, was retained for use as a clubhouse. It was skilfully converted to provide offices, a lounge, and bedrooms for aviators, and became a landmark on the airport.

Below: The formidable sight that confronted the workmen when they arrived to start work. The old allotments had been allowed to become derelict, with huts and rubbish strewn everywhere.

A part of the old town ramparts was scheduled for demolition in the ambitious plan for the airport. Work has just started as this superb aerial view shows.

A tractor starts to clear one of the many hedges on the farm site in preparation for a landing area which was to be eulogised by many experts in the aviation field.

Left: The heavier gear is bought in to the site by the contractors Frank Bevis and Co to remove the Victorian fortifications.

Below: In the background of the little railway constructed to shift spoil is part of the ramparts – remains of Hilsea's military fortifications – which had to be dynamited to make way for the new era of flight.

Left: One of the approach roads takes shape with what looks like sheer hard graft by the workforce.

Below: The airport site is cleared and is ready for the heavy machinery that would eventually level the grass surface to provide access for the aircraft.

Within a month of the start of the work a plane had landed and made history with a first take-off. Flying Officer AL Mortimer, whose parents lived at Southsea, flew in on 14 December, 1930, in an Avro 616 Avian. The following day, joined by city councillor John Webb, he hopped over to Farlington racecourse where he deposited the councillor before flying back to Heston. Flying Officer Mortimer and Councillor Webb are pictured second and third from left before their departure.

Nº 21522

PORTSMOUTH AIRPORT.

OFFICIAL OPENING,

SATURDAY, 2ND JULY, 1932.

This Ticket is issued on the understanding that neither the Corporation nor the Automobile Association accept any responsibility in respect of loss of, or damage to Motor Vehicles or Aircraft, the contents thereof, or for injury to the occupants thereof, or persons visiting the Aerodrome.

ADMISSION **1/=** (Including Tax).

Under no circumstances will money paid for this Ticket be refunded.

Opening day was on 2 July 1932, and came with a blaze of publicity and a huge aerial pageant. More than 50,000 people made their way across what was a still desolate part of the city to watch the official ceremony and an afternoon of flying displays and aerial entertainment.

Below: A group of youngsters crowd the barrier, some pointing skyward, during the events on the opening day

Left: Patriotism was strong in 1932 as the proud Union Jack shows, positioned amongst the spectators.

Below: The actual opening ceremony was undertaken by the Under-secretary for Air, Sir Philip Sassoon, who rather curiously flew into Grange Aerodrome at Gosport, before being escorted to Portsmouth for a celebration lunch at the Guildhall. He is pictured on the dais, surrounded by civic dignitaries, officially opening the new undertaking. (Quadrant – Flight Collection)

A large number of aircraft were present on the opening day and one of the most popular was the Westland-Hill Pterodactyl. Crowds gather around it, resplendent in its prehistoric livery, with eyes that rolled as the plane moved

Left: A Hawker Hart with a shark-like look caused great amusement to spectators young and old on 2 July, 1932. (Quadrant – Flight Collection)

Below: The Armstrong Whitworth Argosy airliner is seen on the right of this picture, waiting to take civic dignitaries on a pleasure flight.

Hawker Furies from Tangmere delighted spectators on the opening day of the municipal aerodrome.

The Hilsea gasworks provide an incongruous backdrop as spectators inspect the line-up of light planes on the opening day.

The Pterodactyl flies in over the heads of a line of spectators after taking part in a balloon-bursting event.

Above: The Cierva C19 autogyro, probably G-ABUC, a forerunner of the modern helicopter, also took part in the fun and games of the opening day.

Left: Civic dignitaries, including the Lord Mayor Ferdinand Foster, are pictured boarding the Armstrong Whitworth Argosy, City of Liverpool, for a sightseeing flight around the skies over Portsmouth.

Flying displays were always a popular event and served to capture the attention of a public that was showing increasing interest in aviation. This stunning view of 1933 shows a line of sightseers at the barrier across the airport while the planes prepare for the show.

Above: The interior of the control tower at Portsmouth, then boasting the most modern equipment.

Opposite page: A staff member signals to an aircraft using an Aldis lamp from the balcony on the top of the control tower.

Above: Ready for any emergency is the Rolls-Royce fire tender, complete with hose and extinguishers.

Below: The two royal Puss Moths stand near the concrete apron at Portsmouth following the departure of the two princes for the dockyard.

Above: On 11 July, 1932, the airport had its first royal visitors when the Prince of Wales (later Edward VIII) and Prince George flew into Portsmouth in two red white and blue Puss Moth aircraft. From the airport they travelled to the dockyard from where they were ferried out to join their father, George V, aboard the Royal Yacht *Victoria & Albert* to visit the home fleet at Weymouth.

A view of early days at the airport with the still-incomplete Eastern Road at the foot of the picture. The word Portsmouth was emblazoned on the airstrip to give visiting pilots a positive destination check.

A Klemm L27A gets its engine up to speed before take-off. This aircraft was first registered in 1931 and flew until 1946 when it was finally scrapped in Wiltshire.

The aircraft manufacturing firm of Airspeed moved from York into purpose-built premises at Portsmouth in 1933. Here workers are pictured taking a break while working on the wing section of an aircraft.

An Airspeed Courier takes shape on the factory floor at Portsmouth.

Another view shows the crowded workshop of the fledgling company.

A complete Courier poses for the camera on the grass airstrip at Portsmouth. The Courier was the first British aircraft to have a retractable undercarriage.

Another Airspeed product, the Oxford, became a staple of RAF training flights. By the end of the Second World War more that 8500 had been built, with more than 4500 coming from Portsmouth. The final one came off the Portsmouth production line on 14 July 1945.

A smart-looking Airspeed Courier G-ACLF, a demonstration model built for RK Dundas, Airspeed's distributor in India, takes a promotional camera call with a contemporary Rolls-Royce.

Above: G-ACLF is made ready for take-off under the watchful eyes of a group of experts.

Left: A Fox Moth pilot prepares to take a young lady passenger aboard at Portsmouth.

Right: The prototype model of another Airspeed baby, the Envoy, is seen at Portsmouth minus its port engine cowling. In the background is a clutch of Furies and Virginias.

Below: Three Vickers Virginias give a display while spectators line the fence watching the giant machines. Note the rear gunner in his precarious position at the tail of the nearest aircraft.

A lazy day's flying at Portsmouth. Pilots and passengers stroll towards the clubhouse – the old Highgrove Farm.

Right: Fox Moth G-ACCA became one of the first airborne delivery vans when special editions of the *Evening News* were flown to the island at the start of Cowes Week in July 1933.

Below: A corner of the airport site on a damp day, with the Airspeed factory on the right of the picture.

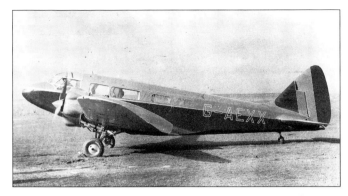

Another of Airspeed's successes was the Envoy, a model that was chosen for service in high places. Here is Series 3 Envoy G-AEXX at Portsmouth, resplendent in the livery of the King's Flight – the colours of the Household Cavalry, which were red, royal blue and silver. The interior was styled by Rumbold and was indeed fit for a king. Young fans could buy a Dinky Toy model of the aircraft, in correct livery, for eight pence (3p).

The prototype three-engine Airspeed ferry was developed for air ace Sir Alan Cobham in 1932. The aircraft, G-ABSI Youth of Britain, was used for the National Aviation Days and by 1935 had flown 1700 hours, made 18,000 landings, and had carried 160,000 passengers. It was later sold to Portsmouth, Southsea and Isle of Wight Aviation.

The elegant Airspeed Viceroy prepares for take-off at Portsmouth. The machine was demonstrated very successfully at the Society of British Aircraft Constructors Show at Hendon on 2 July, 1934.

The stately Ferry G-ACFB coming in at Portsmouth before being sold to Midland and Scottish Air Ferries.

Left: The date is March 1934 and these youngsters wait for a joyride while a member of the ground crew prepares to start the engine.

Below: From 1933 Jersey Airways ran a regular service from Portsmouth to the Channel Islands where their de Havilland Dragons landed on the beach. Here G-ACMP St Aubin's Bay takes on passengers in front of the airport's distinctive picket fence.

Jersey Airways planes line up at Portsmouth, with the former Highgrove Farm building to the right of the picture. In front is a Westland Wessex belonging to Portsmouth, Southsea & Isle of Wight Aviation.

Portsmouth, Southsea & Isle of Wight Aviation commenced services at Portsmouth before the airport was officially opened. This picture by Tunbridge Wells photographer and postcard publisher EA Sweetman shows a portion of the company's fleet at Portsmouth.

Right: This smart Puss Moth – G-ABIY – was also captured on film by Sweetman in a series of pictures depicting the company's fleet.

Below: Westland Wessex G-ABVB gains height in this stunning view as it makes its way to the Isle of Wight. The plane crashed at Ryde on 30 May, 1936, slightly injuring the pilot.

G-ABVB seems a popular subject for the camera as this Sweetman picture of the Wessex high over the packed streets of Southsea shows.

Left: All smiles as joyride passengers step back on to terra firma after a trip into the unknown over Portsmouth and Spithead.

Below: August Bank Holiday was always a popular time for taking a trip, and here passengers are seen embarking at Portsmouth for a day in the Isle of Wight.

FLYING

PLEASURE FLIGHTS—10-MILE CIRCULAR TOUR

FROM PORTSMOUTH OR RYDE AIRPORTS. FARES: 4/6 Adults, 3/- Children.

INCLUSIVE FARE 14/6

AIR & COACH TOUR

GRAND ALL-DAY COACH TOUR ROUND THE ISLE OF WIGHT, WITH FLIGHT TO AND FROM RYDE.

FROM PORTSMOUTH
13/- Single
21/6 Day Return

BOURNEMOUTH

FROM RYDE
9/- Single
15/- Day Return

FROM PORTSMOUTH OR RYDE 19/6

AIR CRUISE ROUND THE I.W.

A 45 minutes flight round the Island coastline.

RYDE

25 SERVICES DAILY.
FARES: 5/- Single
8/6 Day Return
9/6 Period Return
Ask for particulars of Excursion Fares.

4/6 & 7/6

PLEASURE FLIGHTS

10 and 20 MILES
FROM
PORTSMOUTH & RYDE.

SANDOWN

FARES: 8/- Single
12/6 Day Return
15/- Period Return
including Car Service in the Isle of Wight.

FOR 7/6 ONLY!!

TEA
AT THE AIRPORT.

PLEASURE FLIGHT,

CAR SERVICE
TO & FROM SOUTHSEA

FROM PORTSMOUTH
12/9 Single
22/6 Day Return

SOUTHAMPTON

FROM RYDE
7/9 Single
14/- Day Return

CAR SERVICE

BETWEEN
AIRPORT & TOWN STATION,
CLARENCE PIER,
& SOUTH PARADE PIER.

BUS SERVICE

CLARENCE PIER VI. SOUTH PARADE PIER TO THE AIRPORT EVERY HALF-HOUR FROM 9.30 A.M. DAILY.

ISLE OF WIGHT AIR SERVICES.

FULL PARTICULARS from

P.S. & I.O.W. AVIATION LTD.

THE AIRPORT, PORTSMOUTH. 74374.

BOOKING OFFICES:
CLARENCE PIER KIOSK. Tel. 6054.
SOUTH PARADE PIER KIOSK. Tel. 31996.
TOWN STATION KIOSK. Tel. 4266.
RYDE AIRPORT. Tel. Ryde 2277.
SANDOWN AIRPORT. Tel. Sandown 400.

Right: A line-up of Portsmouth, Southsea & Isle of Wight Aviation Airspeed Couriers takes a photo-call at Portsmouth. The Courier was a popular aircraft with a cruising speed of 130mph.

Below: Westland Wessex G-ABVB, one of the Portsmouth, Southsea & Isle of Wight Aviation fleet, in smart livery waits for passengers on the field at Portsmouth.

Southsea postcard publisher Russell captured this picture of a Portsmouth, Southsea & Isle of Wight Aviation de Havilland Dragon G-ACRF en route from Ryde to Portsmouth. This particular craft was sold to Australia in 1936 and gave good service until 1954.

Ready for the honeymoon. Family members and the bridesmaid gather to say *bon voyage* to the happy couple as they board the plane at Portsmouth, bound for the Isle of Wight.

Portsmouth, Southsea & Isle of Wight Aviation Klemm L27 III three-seater G-ABJX is pictured on the apron with the clubhouse in the background.

Above left: The company's Fox Moth biplane, G-ACCA, in its original livery.   *Above right*:   The same aircraft now sporting more fancy paintwork.   Portsmouth, Southsea & Isle of Wight Aviation acquired two Fox Moths at a cost of £1045 each.   The second – G-ACIG – flew on until it was taken over by the RAF in 1940.

De Havilland 60X Moth of Portsmouth, Southsea & Isle of Wight Aviation before the lens at Portsmouth. While being operated by Portsmouth Aero Club this machine crashed at sea at Spithead in 1934 killing both occupants. Originally this aircraft was used for training purposes.

Airspeed Courier G-ADAY in the original livery of Portsmouth, Southsea & Isle of Wight Aviation. This Courier was eventually taken over by the Air Transport Auxiliary for war work and was later scrapped at Portsmouth in 1941.

Another of the company's Couriers – G-ACZL- was impressed into the RAF in 1940 and was damaged beyond repair when it crashed in Essex later in the year.

Newspapers were flown to the Isle of Wight at the time of the 1934 Cup Final, a service that continued for many years.

Service aircraft were a rare sight at Portsmouth. This Handley Page Hampden from No 7 Squadron provided the airport with a military flavour for a short while.

Equally imposing was a Handley Page transport plane which visited in August 1933.

Above: Two French airliners pay a surprise visit to Portsmouth on 18 September 1933.

Left: A French-registered de Havilland Dragon flew in soon afterwards, giving the airport a truly continental air.

Above: The big de Havilland DH86 Express Diana – a four-engine version of the Rapide – comes in to land with the familiar silhouette of the gasworks in the background.

Right: Diana in close-up parked up near the distinctive picket fence of Portsmouth Airport. The Express lived up to its name as at the time it was considered to be the fastest British airliner.

A German Luftwaffe three-engine Junkers was certainly an unusual visitor to Portsmouth in August 1933 – neither country knowing what was to come by 1939.

A Lockheed Vega Gull sports an American-looking shape on the apron at Portsmouth.

A Vickers 259 Viastra with its unusual tailplane formation and huge undercarriage spats.

Portsmouth aviators take a break to watch the arrival of a Short Scion Senior.

Members of the ground crew gather round the Short Scion Senior, with the distinctive shape of an Aeronca in the background.

Pioneer aviatrix Amy Johnson taxis her Avro Avian in on the grass at Portsmouth. Following the break-up of her marriage to air ace Jim Mollison, Amy worked for Portsmouth, Southsea & Isle of Wight Aviation, living at North End in Portsmouth for while. She eventually joined the Air Transport Auxiliary at the outbreak of the Second World War, only to lose her life over the Thames estuary on Sunday 5 January 1941.

Left: Clouds loom over a Ford 5AC-T Trimotor at Portsmouth in August 1934. A few months later this aircraft was sold to Australia. The all-metal Trimotor carried 13 passengers at a cruising speed of 122mph, and a similar model was used by Admiral Richard Byrd in his record-breaking flight over the South Pole in 1929.

Below: The unusual shape of an International Airways Monospar ST10 is captured by the camera. Portsmouth, Southsea & Isle of Wight Aviation flew a number of these craft, one of them – G-ACTS – being the plane that won the King's Cup in 1934.

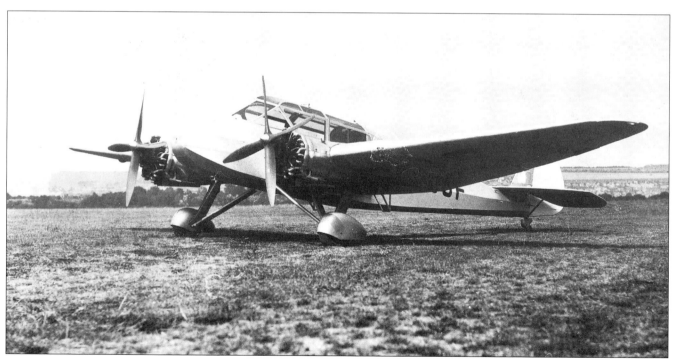

Right: The stubby shape of an Aeronca C3 makes a good subject for the camera as the pilot prepares for takeoff.

Below: The Aeronca comes in to land at Portsmouth at a steep angle as other flyers stop to watch.

Monsieur Henri Mignet demonstrates his brainchild – the Flying Flea – against the background of Portsdown Hill in August 1935. More than 10,000 people flocked to the airport to see the tiny machine which was powered by a two-stroke motorcycle engine and could be built for about £70. The hapless M Mignet was forced to make a run for it after the end of his demonstration to avoid autograph hunters.

Snouty RAF Heyford bombers await orders at Portsmouth.

Left: In November 1935 a young man passed through Portsmouth Airport with an unusual request. The 19-year-old Roy Gropler had recently arrived in the UK by sea and had purchased a Klemm monoplane for £350. He stopped at Portsmouth to have extra fuel tanks fitted and to have the name of his lady love painted on the side of his plane. She was a young Gosport girl called Terry Shone whom he had met on the sea journey from Australia. Gropler left Portsmouth on 10 November with just a tin of biscuits, two gallons of water and £7 in cash, and courageously flew solo to Adelaide in 149hr 15min and on into the Australian aviation history books. Sadly Gropler died in a plane crash at Parafield just three years later.

Right: May of the next year saw a visit by glamour boy of the air, birdman Clem Sohn. More than 65,000 people travelled to Portsmouth to see the early sky-diver give a display. Sohn performed his act dressed in an all-white flying suit which was fitted with bat wings. Thick cloud delayed his show until late evening and on his descent he was blown off course and ended up with his parachute caught in the trees at the edge of the airfield.

Right: One of the earliest aircraft hijackings took place at Portsmouth in August 1936 when two Airspeed employees stole a Courier G-ACVE with the intention of flying it to Spain where the civil war had just started. They were tempted by the reports of high wages, but as neither man could fly the story inevitably had an unhappy ending. The plane crashed into the ramparts at the north of the field, just east of the railway line, killing one of the pair. The other was sentenced to four months' jail.

Below: Jersey Airways' Dragon St Owen's Bay looks trim on the grass at Portsmouth.

Instructor and pupil are ready to take to the air in Portsmouth Aero Club's Miles Hawk Major G-ADMW in 1934.

A de Havilland Dragon belonging to Railway Air Services is given a helping hand from ground crew on take-off. Railway Air Services was formed from the major rail companies and Imperial Airways. RAS delivered the first air mail to Somerton Aerodrome in the Isle of Wight on 21 August 1934. After refuelling the Dragon brought back 2,500 letters to the mainland.

The Westland Wessex trimotor G-EBXK used by air ace Sir Alan Cobham on his Cobham Air Routes Channel Islands service. The service was short-lived however, for after the loss of an aircraft and its pilot, the business was sold to Olley Air Service.

Opposite page: On 29 September 1936, Portsmouth was put in the spotlight when the England–Johannesburg air race started. The South African magnate Isaac W Schlesinger had put up the £10,000 prize money and Portsmouth was chosen for the start because of its excellent grass surface. Disaster struck a week before the race had even started when Tom Campbell Black lost his life in an accident at Liverpool's Speke Airport. The irony was that Campbell Black's Percival Mew Gull had only been taken north to be officially christened Miss Liverpool. Other withdrawals meant that of the original 14 entrants only nine started. Popular flyers CWA Scott, right, and Giles Guthrie are pictured arriving for the race.

Above: Scott and Guthrie pose with their Percival Vega Gull, No 6 in the race, for the cameraman. No 6 was the only aircraft to finish the race, coming across the line in a time of 52 hours, 56 minutes.

England–Johannesburg air race entrants.

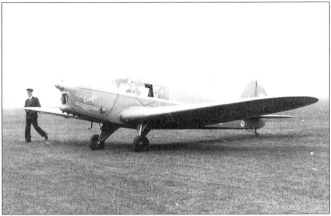

Entrant No 7 was DW Llewellyn's smart Percival Vega Gull.

Lt PA Booth gets a helping hand with his BA Eagle, No 10, on the grass at Portsmouth.

Flight-Lt Rose's BA4 Double Eagle, No 4, stands on the apron before the race.

England–Johannesburg air race entrants.

Above: No 8 is AE Clouston's Miles Hawk VI.

Left: At the front of the numbering is Major Miller's Percival Mew Gull.

England–Johannesburg air race entrants.

Above: Another smart Mew Gull is Capt Halse's No 2.

Right: Finally No 3, Victor Smith's Miles Sparrow Hawk, gets a last-minute check-up.

Ken Waller, left, and Captain Maxwell Findlay pose with the ill-fated G-AENA Gabrielle before the Portsmouth–Johannesburg race. Waller and the engineer CD Peachey survived the crash at Abercorn, while Findlay and radio operator AH Morgan lost their lives. (Quadrant – Flight Collection)

The Airspeed Envoy Gabrielle, No 13 in the race, gets a helping hand from members of the ground crew.
(Quadrant – Flight Collection)

Early-morning floodlights illuminate the scene as spectators gather on the morning of 29 September 1936 to see the competitors take to the skies. Nearest the camera is No 6, the only plane to have finished the course.

A glider soars in over Portsmouth Airport in this sombre picture from 1937.

Left: De Havilland Albatross airliner waits for passengers with its door open near the departure area at Portsmouth.

Below: At the end of the war things slowly returned to normal, and in May 1947 the ban on private flying was finally lifted. The city's aero club celebrated with an air display, supported by aircraft from many other south-coast clubs. (Quadrant – Flight Collection)

Right: Portsmouth, Southsea & Isle of Wight Aviation was restructured as Portsmouth Aviation in 1943 and aimed to go into production with a revolutionary light aircraft called the Aerocar. The prototype G-AGTG flew in June 1947, but because of the economic climate production never commenced and it became the only one produced.

Below: Spreading the word with a wing and a prayer is this Miles M65 Gemini of the Missionary Air Force. This plane was brand new at the show in 1947, but was sadly lost in the Belgian Congo the following year.

You could learn to fly at the airport in this smart Cessna belonging to Portsmouth Flying School.

A Channel Airways Douglas DC3 is pictured at Portsmouth in the mid 1950s, at a time that the airport was coming into its own and was beginning to show a profit. (Portsmouth City Museum)

Left: Two smart air hostesses pose in front of a Channel Airways DC3 at Portsmouth in the heyday of commercial flight.

Below: The service engineer is on site maintaining the pumps which provide the aviation fuel that keeps the aircraft in the air. (Peter Rogers)

This page and opposite: These five pictures eloquently depict the events that led to the change in Portsmouth Airport's fortunes. On 15 August 1967 – a day blessed with torrential rain – the first mishap occurred. A Hawker Siddeley 748 turboprop with only 17 passengers and four crew was due in from Southend, after which it was to fly to Paris. The grass runway was slick with rain and the 748 slewed to the left on landing, the undercarriage collapsed and the plane ended up with its nose buried in a grass bank. To add to the problem, ninety minutes later the event was repeated when another 748 from the Channel Islands touched down, ran off the runway towards the Eastern Road, slammed through the concrete and wire fence, and finished up with its belly across the Eastern Road. The Board of Trade subsequently ruled that the runways were too short, which effectively banned the 748s from using the city, so Channel Airways re-routed their services to Eastleigh, thus sealing Portsmouth airport's fate.

This page and opposite: By now Airspeed had become part of the de Havilland empire and the manufacture of quality aircraft continued at Portsmouth as these two pictures show.

Hawker Siddeley Aviation eventually brought de Havilland into its fold as these brand-new headquarters buildings at Portsmouth show.

No. **3101**

Portsmouth Aero Club Ltd.
Telephone 717641.

Pleasure Flight Ticket **10/-**
INCLUDING MONTHLY MEMBERSHIP.

THIS TICKET, AVAILABLE FOR ONE FLIGHT
is issued subject to the conditions laid out on the reverse.

GREETINGS FROM THE PORTSMOUTH AERO CLUB

The Portsmouth Aero Club sent its greetings by way of this effective postcard featuring Auster Alpha G-AJAB.

Airport visitors gather round a de Havilland Hornet Moth, part of the display of vintage aircraft held at the airport on 15 April 1968.

Bucker BU131 G-ATJX is one of a number of aircraft from an earlier period visiting Portsmouth in a 1968 rally organised by the Portsmouth Electricity Flying Club.

The date is 12 May 1969, and an RAF Andover comes in to land. This aircraft, the military version of the ill-fated HS 748s which crashed, was the largest plane to visit Portsmouth since the Board of Trade restrictions were imposed.

This stunning aerial view from 1970 shows clearly how the airport had expanded since its inception. The Eastern Road is complete, although the flyover was then not yet built. The packed homes at Highbury, Drayton and Cosham eloquently depict the growth of a great city.

Left: JF Airlines took delivery of its first Twin Pioneer on 31 March 1971, at a ceremony attended by the Lord Mayor of Portsmouth, Jonathan Blair, and promised great things for the company and for the city.

Inset below left: In September 1971 JF Airlines scored a major coup when a million-dollar Russian jet airliner dropped in to be evaluated by the company. The Yak-40 short-haul 40-seater aircraft was owned by Italian air-taxi company Aertirrena, and was piloted by a former Italian Air Force pilot Sergio Sette and by Signora Fiorenza de Barnardi, then one of only two Italian women to hold a commercial pilot's licence. Captain Sette is pictured right with co-pilot de Barnardi in the centre in front of the jet.

Below: Up, up and away and the Yak-40 takes off from Portsmouth after its brief stay.

In October 1971 a film star visited the airport – not the flesh-and-blood type but an old Stringbag. The last Fairey Swordfish flying was featured in the hit movie *Sink the Bismarck*, and is pictured here at Portsmouth with its pilot Lt-Commander Paddy Carr, and his crew Alan Hyde and Lawrence Turner.

Above left and right: Two of JF Airlines' Twin Pioneers – G-APHX and G-APHY – take camera calls in 1972 at Portsmouth in their new livery as Jersey Ferry Airlines. Both aircraft were eventually sold to Kuwait.

Regular readers of *The News* had no need to miss out while on holiday in the Channel Islands in 1972. JF Airlines won the contract to deliver copies along with passengers, who are getting an early view of the current happenings as they wait to board their aircraft for a June holiday.

Eighteen-year-old Joanne enjoys her precarious perch atop the wing of a Tiger Moth as the Barnstormers give one of their thrilling displays at Portsmouth in August 1972. The next year the aircraft was destroyed in a collision with another plane at Tollerton.

Above: A campaign to save the airport was launched in May 1973 by the Portsmouth Airport Users Association, which hoped to get 10,000 names on a petition – equal to one for every take-off and landing at the airport in 1972. Campaigners are pictured in the streets of the city encouraging residents to support their cause.

Above: Don't lose your way! The airport directory was still a useful help for visitors to the site.

Right: On a cold 31 December 1973, hundreds of people made their way to the airport to witness the end of an era on the final official day of flying. Scores of light planes flew in to let pilots and passengers take part in a day of nostalgia and to say farewell to a popular aviation venue.

The sun was setting on Portsmouth Airport in more ways than one. This moody picture was taken at a quiet corner just before the last aircraft finally left.

In August 1980 the airport site assumed a new role – that of a pop concert venue. The organisers expected many thousands of fans to congregate on the city to see a country-and-western extravaganza headlined by Johnny Cash and Glenn Campbell. In the event only a tiny percentage of the expected number turned up, and they can be seen gathered around the stage in this unusual aerial view.

Although the airport was officially closed, on 16 February 1974, Harold Wilson, then leader of the Labour Party, arrived by helicopter to speak in the city and at Gosport. He was met by the MP for Portsmouth West, Frank Judd, now Lord Judd of Portsea.

The houses of the Anchorage Park development begin to spread across the redundant airport site, finally to obliterate what once was the city's great dream.